A Kalmus Classic Edition

Mathilde

MARCHESI

TWENTY-FOUR VOCALISES

Opus 2

FOR SOPRANO OR MEZZO SOPRANO

K 09169

Kalmus

Nº 1. Swelling and diminishing upon a tone.

(Messa di voce.)

MATHILDE CASTRONE MARCHESI. Op. 2.

Nº 2. Portamento.

Andante e molto legato.

Nº 3. Portamento.

Sostenuto molto.

Nº 4. Smooth, even singing.
(Canto spianato.)

Nº 5. Smooth, even singing.
(Canto spianato.)

Nº 6. Diatonic Scale.

№ 7. Diatonic Scale.

Nº 8. Diatonic Scale.

Moderato.

Nº 9. Diatonic Scale, with dotted notes.

Nº 1C. Quatrains.

(4-measure phrases.)

Allegro giusto.

№ 11. Chromatic Scale.

No. 12. Chromatic Scale.

Nº 13. Theme with variations.

№ 13. Minor Scales.

Nº 14. Repeated notes.

№ 15. Triplets.

Allegretto.

№ 16. Arpeggios.

Nº 17. The long and short appoggiatura.

№ 18. Gruppetto and Mordente.

Nº 19. Syncopation.

Allegro giusto.

Nº 20. Detached and accented notes.

Nº 21. Large Skips.
(Salti.)

Nº 22. Shake.

(Trillo.)

№ 23. 1st Recapitulation.
(1er Résumé.)

Nº 24. 2nd Recapitulation.
IIe Résumé.)